6/2

South Woodham Ferrers

A Pictorial History

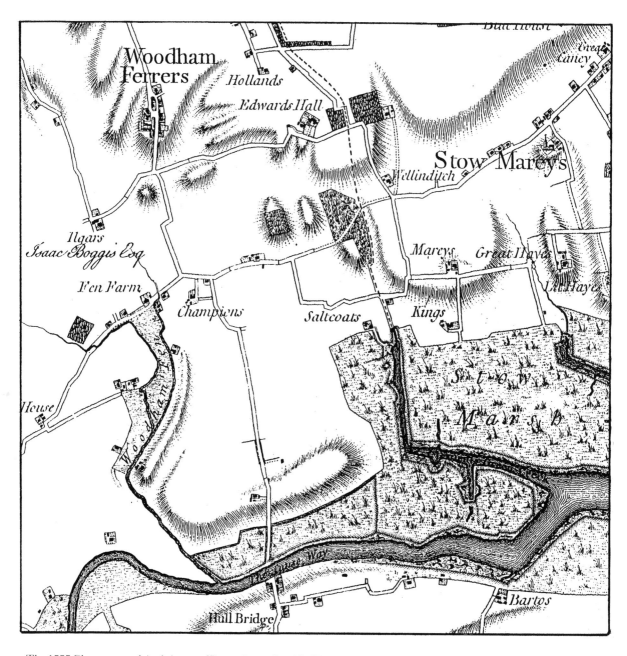

The 1777 Chapman and André map of Essex shows the old village of Woodham Ferrers with the South Woodham Ferrers peninsula indicated as an area of widely scattered buildings and grazing marsh.

South Woodham Ferrers
A Pictorial History

John Frankland

Phillimore

1992

Published by
PHILLIMORE & CO. LTD.
Shopwyke Hall, Chichester, Sussex

© South Woodham Ferrers Local History Society, 1992

ISBN 0 85033 832 8

Printed and bound in Great Britain by
BIDDLES LTD.
Guildford, Surrey

In memory of
L. J. 'Jack' Holden
(1918-1990)

List of Illustrations

Frontispiece: Chapman & André map, 1777

Acknowledgements

I am grateful for the inspiration of friend and former colleague John Fisher and for the support offered by my fellow Local History Society committee members Roger Bennett, Lynn French and Bill Thomas. On behalf of the society I would especially like to thank the South Woodham Ferrers Town Council for its valued support during the preparation of the book. Photographic work has been expertly dealt with by Geoff Frankland, Lynn French, Pete Rogers and Paul Skeet whose enthusiasm and skill have been greatly appreciated.

Illustration Acknowledgements

The following photographs are reproduced by kind permission of the Anglican Congregation of Holy Trinity Church, 106; Mrs. L. Barber, 112, 121, 139, 166; Mrs. W. Beavins, 18, 116, 130, 132, 136, 141; Mr. H. 'Joe' Coward, 6, 11, 12, 14, 15, 46, 47, 114, 119, 153, 156, 161, 162, 163; Mr. J. Coward, 45, 115, 140, 143; Mr. A. Deavin, 1, 2, 20, 126, 158, 159; Essex Record Office, 3, 7, 39, 53, 55, 105, 150; Mrs. B. Holden, 54, 127, 134, 146, Mr. E. Holden, 113; Mr. L. Holden, 16, 22, 133; Mr. V. Holden, 160; Mr. & Mrs. D. Hunt, 57, 58; *Maldon and Burnham Standard*, 169; Mr. A. Mandara, 61; The Maldon Museum Collection, 17; Mr. P. Milton, County Planner, Essex County Council, 56, 59, 62-66, 69-71, 73-75, 77-79, 81-83, 85, 86, 88, 89, 91, 92, 94-96, 97, 125, 128, 129, 157, 165, 170-173, 181, 182; Network SouthEast, 24; Ordnance Survey, 68, 72, 76, 80, 84, 87, 90, 93 (with present day maps redrawn by the author); Mr. L. H. Oxley, 23, 29; Mr. W. W. Pepper, 120, 123; Phillimore & Co., Frontis; Mr. D. Potter, 26, 27; Public Record Office, 2 (document E31/1 f.57); Mrs. R. Ralston, 52, 98, 107-109, 117, 131, 137, 145; Chairman of the Village Hall Management Committee, Mr. I Roberts, 99; Mr. R. Smith, 40, 44; Southend Aerial Photographs, 167, 168; South Woodham Garage, 135; South Woodham Women's Institute, 118; Mr. and Mrs. A. Stout, 13, 152, 154; the Michael Turner Collection, 102; *The Whalebone*, 48, 49, 50, 101; Mr. T. Williams, 28, 30, 31, 33, 34, 35-38. All other photographs are from the collection of the South Woodham Ferrers Local History Society.

Finally I must thank Janet for her patience and support, and Rebecca and Timothy for not interrupting too often.

Foreword

It is usual for an author of a work of this nature to be able to claim a personal acquaintance with his subject since childhood days. I have to admit that I cannot do this. My first encounter with the area was in the late 1960s when I recall following an Ordnance Survey map expecting to find a usable crossing of the River Crouch at the site marked 'ford' and 'ferry' which, upon reflection, was at South Woodham Ferrers. On that occasion a high tide soon dismissed any thoughts of using the ford and I subsequently discovered that I had missed the last ferry by about 20 years.

A more formal introduction to the area came in 1972 when I took up employment in Essex and in the two decades since that time South Woodham Ferrers, as a growing new town, must have been one of the most studied, surveyed and photographed places in Essex. However, I am sure that older residents will forgive me for suggesting that in its earlier form it was not the obvious destination for photographers seeking a village in which to practise their art. Consequently there was no single source or collection of photographs on which this book could be based and even the helpful staff of the Essex Record Office were not able to produce more than a handful of relevant illustrations.

That this book has become a reality therefore is largely due to the generosity of South Woodham Ferrers residents and ex-residents who have kindly loaned their treasured photographs to be copied over the past 20 years or so. Many of these people have been happy to share not only their photographs but also their memories of old South Woodham Ferrers with me and with other members of the South Woodham Ferrers Local History Society and I am very grateful to all who have helped in this way. I would particularly like to thank Les Holden, author of that very readable and colourful account of South Woodham's early days 'Where's Woodham Ferris?', for commenting upon the draft manuscript and for patiently dealing with my many questions.

I trust that all those who have helped in any way will see this book as a fitting tribute to the old South Woodham Ferrers that many of them knew and loved.

In the text which follows readers will note that the name South Woodham Ferrers was not formally used until 1913 when, apart from the addition of the word 'South', 'Ferrers' – as opposed to the corrupt form 'Ferris' – was re-adopted. It was thought to be an unnecessary complication to switch between the Ferris and Ferrers versions depending on whether the particular subject matter fell before or after that date. Therefore the present day version has been used throughout except where proper names (e.g. Woodham Ferris Brick Co.) are referred to. In fact, the word 'Ferrers' has been omitted from formal titles for many years (e.g. South Woodham Smallholders & Social Society) and this more manageable form has sometimes been used in the following pages where flow of the text has seemed to warrant it.

WOODHAM·FERRERS - 1763

Fred Spatch
Photo
Chelmsford
Copyrig

1. South Woodham Ferrers derived its name from Woodham Ferrers, pictured here at the turn of the century. In terms of topography, origins and development the two settlements could hardly present greater contrasts.

Introduction

Early History, the Manors and Farms

South Woodham Ferrers is largely a product of the 20th century. Indeed, so recent are its origins that it was not until 1913 that the name South Woodham Ferrers was formally adopted to identify the settlement emerging in the southern part of Woodham Ferrers parish as being separate from the original village of Woodham Ferrers, one mile to the north.

The name Woodham is said to derive from two Saxon words, 'wuda' meaning a wood and 'ham' meaning a farm or homestead. In order to distinguish this manor from the nearby Woodham Mortimer and Woodham Walter, the family name of Henry de Ferrers, the manor's first Norman lord, was adopted.

At the southern edge of the manor, where the low-lying land is embraced on three sides by the tidal waters of the River Crouch and the two creeks of Fenn Creek and Clementsgreen Creek, is the area now known as South Woodham Ferrers.

2. Woodham Ferrers was an old market town and its High Street is fronted by buildings dating back to the 16th and 17th centuries. In contrast, South Woodham Ferrers in the valley below is largely a product of the 20th century.

·henric·

Tč . ii . fot . nī . i . Silū . cl . poč . lx . ač . ṕa . tč . 9n̄ rec̄ . dim̄ moł nī . īi . Sēp ē ibi

. i . pbr . Tč . yii . anim̄ . 7 . xl . oił . 7 lx . poč . 7 . i . rund̄ . m̄ . xyiii . anim̄ .

7 . cxl . oił . 7 . lxxx . poč . 7 . i . rund̄ . Tč . uał . x . lib̄ . m̄ . xii . 7 in cēṕ rex

. ē . ṡū cā́i ṡimilē 7 tantū ualuī q̄n̄ recp̄.

¶ Ḃund de Wibriceṡḣama Steplam tenc̄ . h . in dn̄io qđ tenuit Bondiˀ

lib hō . ẻ . ř . ē . ṕ oñ . 7 ṕ . iii . ḣid̄ . 7 . dim̄ . Sēp . ii . boȗ . tč . iiii . ṡer̄ . m̄ . iii . Sēp . i .

car̄ in dn̄io . 7 . dim̄ car̄ hom̄ . tč . c . oił . m̄ . cxxx . Vat ṡep̄ . lx . ṡot.

¶ Ḃund de Celmereṡfoꝛt Vdeham tenc̄ . h . in dn̄io qđ tenuit

Ḃundiˀ ṕ uno mañ . 7 . ṕ xiiii . ḣid̄ Sēp . xxiiii . uilt . tč . yiii . boȗ . m̄ . xxxi .

tč . yi . ṡer̄ . m̄ . iiii . Sēp . iii . car̄ in dn̄io . 7 . xyi . car̄ hom̄ . Silū dccc . poč .

m̄ . i . moł . Tč rec̄ xx . anim̄ . 7 xiii . rund̄ . 7 . ccc . oił 7 . lx . poč . m̄ xxyiii .

anim̄ . 7 . xy . rund̄ . 7 . ccc . oił . 7 . c . poč . 7 . xxxy . cap̄ tč uał . xx . lib̄ . m̄

xxyiii.

¶ Cingam tenc̄ dapifer ḣanꝛa de eo qđ tenuit Ḃondiˀ ṕ oñ . 7 . ṕ y .

ḣid̄ir . 7 . dim̄ . tč . yi . uilt . m̄ . iiii . tč . yiii . boȗ . m̄ . xii . tč . iiii . ṡer̄ . m̄ . iii .

Sēp . ii . car̄ in dn̄io . 7 . iiii . car̄ hom̄ . Silū . d . poč . ḷaṡt . c . oił . tč . xx .

anim̄ . 7 . l . poč . 7 lx . oił . m̄ . yii . añ . 7 . c . oił . 7 . xl . poč . Sēp uał . yii .

lib.

Hundred of CHELMSFORD

4   Henry holds WOODHAM (Ferrers) in lordship, which Bondi held as
    one manor, for 14 hides.
        Always 24 villagers. Then 8 smallholders, now 31; then 6 slaves,
        now 4. Always 3 ploughs in lordship; 16 men's ploughs.
        Woodland, 800 pigs; now 1 mill. Then he acquired 20 cattle,
        13 cobs, 300 sheep and 60 pigs; now 28 cattle, 15 cobs,
        300 sheep, 100 pigs and 35 goats.
    Value then £20; now [£] 28.

---

3.   The landholdings of Henry de Ferrers recorded in the 1086 Domesday Survey include
Woodham Manor, here referred to as 'Udeham' (centre).

Earliest recorded human activity in this area is associated with these two tidal inlets. In the fields at the head of Clementsgreen Creek can be seen a series of 'redhills', the remains of an Iron Age or Roman salt extraction industry whilst Fenn Creek, further upstream, has proved to be a rich source of archaeological finds in recent years. In 1977, for example, two Iron Age human skulls were found in the bed of the creek and subsequent investigations nearby identified evidence of what appeared to be a marshland causeway from the same era. Notwithstanding the interest generated by these finds, in 1983 the discovery on a bank of Fenn Creek of a salt extraction hearth was particularly significant. Late Bronze Age implements associated with this site identified it as the earliest, positively dated salt extraction site in this part of the country. To archaeologists it represented a notable advance in the history of salt working in south-east England.

Earliest documentary evidence of the history of the area is provided by the Domesday entry for the wider area of the manor of Woodham, or 'Udeham' as it was then written. The entry tells us that in the year of the survey, 1086, there were in the manor 24 villagers or 'villeins', the highest class of dependent peasantry holding perhaps 30 acres each, 31 smallholders or 'bordars' who were of lesser standing than the villeins and four slaves. Woodham's total population would have been in the region of 250-300 people which represented an increase of more than 50 per cent in the 20 years since 1066. This was a markedly higher increase than many of the neighbouring manors and was reflected in the manor's value which leapt from £20 to £28 in the same period. We may surmise therefore that, for whatever reason, Woodham was experiencing something of a boom in the early years of William the Conqueror's reign.

The Domesday Survey refers only to the single manor of Woodham; the manors of Champions and Ayotts (or Eyotts), which covered much of the area that was to become South Woodham Ferrers, appear to be post-Domesday growths.

A more detailed survey of the manor of Woodham Ferrers has survived from 1582 to provide us with a vivid description of the riverside rural area. The mix of agriculture and river-related activities which this survey describes suggests that Elizabethan Woodham was, or at least had been, a manor of some diversity. Particular mention is made of the two creeks or 'wharfes' which, it relates, are 'very fytt and dayley used' for the transporting of goods such as butter, cheese, wood, corn and salt 'to and from the cytie of London and els where'.[1] Near these creeks it is recorded that there were oyster lanes, fisheries and salt workings.

The farming activities of the manor had once supported a weekly market and annual sheep fair, which had been granted to the manor by Henry III in 1234. The market and associated activities were clearly related to the more elevated part of the manor where Woodham Ferrers village became established. The area to the south adjacent to the river and creeks where our interest lies was an area of farmland and grazing marsh.

The 1582 survey, like Domesday before it, related to the manor of Woodham itself rather than to the particular area now occupied by the town. It is the two subordinate manors of Champions and Eyotts which are more specifically related to today's town area. It is not certain when these manors came into existence, although their names at least can be traced back to the 14th century. Morant in his *History and Antiquities of the County of Essex* recorded that 'William Champeyne, who dyed in 1356, held, with Alice his wife, a maner called Champaynes'[2] and it seems that it was from this family that the manor took its name. Eyotts is probably associated with the family of William Ayote, reference to whom can be traced back to 1329.

The manor of Woodham fferrwrs als fferys is an anncyente manor of it selfe havinge a leete or viewe of ffranke pledge to it p^{e}r^{t}eynynge & a p^{a}r^{k}e lately disp^{a}r^{k}ed And the same was somtyme p^{a}r^{c}ell of the possessyons of the righte honorable Thomas Audeley of the righte honorable order of the garter knighte late lorde Audeley of Walden & late lorde channcellor of Inglande & before p^{a}r^{c}ell of the possessyons of Henry somtyme marques Dorcett after Duke of Suff^{o}lk and nowe p^{a}r^{c}ell of the possessyons of Robert Audeley Esquire sonne and heire of Thomas Audeley of Derechurche in the Countie of Essex Esquire Nephewe of the said Thomas late lorde Audeleye, beynge situate in the said p^{a}r^{i}she of Woodham fferrys in the said countie of Essex & in the uttermoste p^{a}r^{t}e towards the Southe of the hundred of Chelmesfforde in the saide Countie Adioynynge uppon the hundrethe of Rocheforde in the same countie beynge in a Countrie verye well stored w^{t}he wood, water, meadowe, pasture & corne soyle & havinge verye nere thereunto two wharfes or ...

4. The 1582 Survey of Woodham Manor, preserved in the Essex Record Office, gives a detailed description of this rural riverside manor and the activities of its inhabitants, during the reign of Elizabeth I.

Chapman and André's map of 1777 shows that Champions Farm provided the dominant grouping of farm building in the area and the acreage figures found in the tithe award map some 60 years later confirm that this farm was indeed pre-eminent among the farms in the southern part of the parish. Consequently its fortunes would have influenced as well as reflected the prosperity of the area as a whole.

The schedule accompanying the 1838 tithe map records that the farm extended to 549 acres and that arable fields made up almost 90 per cent of the farmed land on the estate. This was a pattern that was mirrored in the remainder of the farms in the area; arable land predominated but in each case a small portion of pasture had been retained immediately adjacent to the main farm buildings.

Whilst Champions Farm comprised over half the area occupied by the present-day town, most of the remaining land was in the hands of four owners. Eyotts Farm, the largest of the other units, occupied 203 acres in the south-western sector of the town and was one of two farms owned and farmed by James Pertwee, the other being a landholding centred on Fenn Farm and Shaw Farm. Another member of the Pertwee family, John, owned the 181-acre Hamberts Farm which straddled the Wickford – Burnham road to the north, whilst the smaller holdings of Peatlands and Saltcoats were owned by the Rev. Charles Bowden and the Drapers' Company respectively.

The residue of landholdings in the 1838 survey were of 20 acres or less and included the 'Whalebone' land and Charity Field, the latter held by the trustees of Gooses Charity which existed to help the poor of the parish.

This survey undoubtedly coincided with one of the most prosperous periods for farming in the Woodham area. Demand for grain remained high and the country's Corn Laws remained in force to provide protection for British agriculture. However the Anti-Corn Law League was founded in 1839 and within seven years the Corn Laws had been repealed by Robert Peel's Tory government, thus opening the way to greatly increased foreign competition. Coupled with the loss of protection were the effects of improved marine engineering, which enabled the new American prairies to be exploited to the full, and a series of disastrous harvests in England.

In relatively marginal agricultural areas like Woodham the effects at a local level must have been traumatic. Farm values slumped and in the 30 years after 1850 the parish lost one third of its population as people migrated to the towns.

It was an indication of the difficulties facing farming in the locality that, in 1893, it was 'by order of the mortgagees'[3] that Champions Farm was put on the market. By this time only about half of the farm remained as arable fields and the rental value had fallen from £500 to £250 in four decades.

Although farming fortunes were low in the latter half of the 19th century there was the prospect, after years of decline, of an improvement because in 1889 the Great Eastern Railway Company opened a railway line to serve the area. In fact the station at Woodham had been built on land acquired from Champions Farm itself and the possible advantages of the line in respect of enlarged and more accessible markets were obvious.

1.   F. G. Emmison, 'Survey of the Manor of Woodham Ferrers 1582', *Transactions of the Essex Archaeological Society*, vol. XXIV, p.7.
2.   Rev. P. Morant, *The History and Antiquities of the County of Essex*, vol. II, p.32 (1768).
3.   *Champions Farm*, sales catalogue (1893). Essex Record Office reference (hereinafter E.R.O.), B2458.

5. The moated 18th-century Champions Hall once stood at the centre of a complex of farm buildings. Although stripped of its agricultural purpose by the plot division of its lands in the late 1890s, the building was retained as a private residence, as in this inter-war view, and later as a country club.

6. Champions Hall in 1968 still enjoyed some of its original open farmland aspect. The timber-framed building is now a Grade II listed building, but came close to being demolished for development when the estate which now almost surrounds it was proposed.

At the very low upset price of £4,500—about £8 10s. per Acre.

WOODHAM FERRIS;

ESSEX.

Valuable Freehold Estate,

LAND-TAX REDEEMED.

PARTICULARS AND CONDITIONS OF SALE

OF

A VALUABLE FREEHOLD ESTATE

KNOWN AS

"CHAMPIONS FARM,"

Situated in the Parish of Woodham Ferris, close to Woodham Railway Station, on the G.E.R. from London to Burnham and Southminster, Eight Miles from the town and port of Maldon, and Nine Miles from the market town of Chelmsford. It comprises a

COMFORTABLE RESIDENCE, WITH HOMESTEAD,

THREE COTTAGES,

2 Cottages & Farm Premises, & 2 Cottages, with Yard, Barn, & Shed

ONE COTTAGE, TWO WHARVES,

AND ABOUT

531 acres   1 rood   37 poles

OF

GOOD CORN GROWING ARABLE & PASTURE LAND

In the occupation of Mr. WALTER CATCHPOLE,

At the Annual Rent of £250;

Which will be Sold by Auction, by

MESSRS. G. B. HILLIARD & SON

By order of the Mortgagees,

At the Mart, Tokenhouse Yard, London, E.C.,

On THURSDAY, MAY 25, 1893,

At Two o'clock precisely.

Particulars and Conditions of Sale may be obtained of Messrs. Sandilands & Co., 12 Fenchurch-Avenue, Fenchurch-Street, London, E.C.; and of the Auctioneers, Chelmsford.

---

7. The 1893 sale of Champions Farm marked the beginning of the end of the farm as an agricultural unit. It was indicative of the problems facing agriculture at this time that this sale was brought about 'by order of the Mortgagees'.

8.   Eyotts farmhouse, which was predominantly an early 19th-century structure, has been completely rebuilt since this photograph was taken in the 1970s. The red brick cladding, now entirely removed, was a cosmetic feature and did not form part of the original building.

9. Saltcoats farmhouse, pictured here between the wars, was demolished when the sports facilities at Saltcoats Park were built. It was the last in a succession of Saltcoats farmhouses on this and an adjacent site, which derived their name from the salt workings in the area.

10. Part of the landholding of Hamberts Farm, on the northern edge of today's town, once lay within the area of Champions Farm. The farmhouse can be traced back to the early 1700s.

11. One of the many inter-war poultry farms in South Woodham Ferrers was at York House on the Eyotts Estate, where this picture was taken in the 1930s. T. J. Brown & Son of Rayleigh were corn chandlers who used the ford at Hullbridge to deliver feed to South Woodham's poultry farms.

12. Farmworker Eddie Lazell is seen at work in about 1934 near York Road on the Eyotts Estate. By this time the plotland estate roads, originally just staked lines in fields, were defined by well established hedgerows.

13. A smallholding immediately south of the railway station belonged to Henry Smith (right), seen here with other family members in about 1914. The Smith family went on to establish a number of nursery businesses which are still run by the same family today.

14. The hard-working Nobby and Peggy are helping to undersow a barley crop with clover in a field off Hullbridge Road near Green Lane. The land in South Woodham Ferrers produced a wide variety of crops in the 1950s.

15. Nobby and Peggy again; this time baulking a potato field on Ministry land to the east of Hullbridge Road near St Mary's church, in the 1950s.

16. Fred Carter pauses from doing battle with the stiff clay soil at Broughton Farm in about 1918. Although this particular field was being prepared for an arable crop, the farm, originally part of Champions Farm, was run as a successful dairy farm by Fred Carter and his successor Ralph Burchell in the 1920s and 1930s.

Railway, River and Roads

17. At Woodham Ferrers station in about 1910 the requirements of the photographer clearly took precedence over the directions of the stationmaster for this crew member on an eastward bound passenger train.

The railway reached this part of Essex at quite a late stage in the development of the county's rail network. Main lines to the county town of Chelmsford and to Southend opened in 1843 and 1856 respectively but Woodham lies between these two lines and was not an obvious route to any destination sought by the pioneering railway companies.

Prior to the Great Eastern Railway line becoming a reality there had been a number of proposals which, if realised, would have penetrated this sector of the county. The Eastern Counties Railway extensions promoted in 1856 envisaged an ambitious route between Pitsea and Maldon that crossed the River Crouch with what was apparently a combined road and rail bridge at a site immediately south of today's town. Another project that would have served Woodham was the locally sponsored South Essex Railway laid before parliament in 1865 but its promoters were unable to raise the finance necessary to further their aims.

It was to be the early 1880s before the Great Eastern Railway Company found itself in a position where its own proposals could be pursued. Upon publication of the proposed route, spontaneous petitions of support arrived from places which stood to benefit from the lines. Handbills and advertisements in county papers drew support from Woodham to an 'influential and spirited' meeting held in Southminster to show support for the company's proposals.[1] Central to the argument in favour of the line was the beneficial effect that the railway would bring to agriculture and market gardening in the Dengie Peninsula through which the line would run.

The lines promoted by the Great Eastern Railway Company in 1883 became known as the New Essex Lines and provided links from Shenfield to Wickford and from Wickford to Southend with branch lines to Southminster and Maldon, the latter two lines forming a junction at Woodham Ferrers. The primary aim of the Great Eastern Railway Company's proposals was undoubtedly to gain access to the lucrative Southend traffic which at that time relied solely on the southerly route operated by the rival London, Tilbury and Southen Railway Company. Whether the branch lines were, in effect, a favour to help gain parliamentary acceptance of a rival Southend route is difficult to tell at this distance in time. Local concerns that the company might implement the Southend route but not the branch lines were sufficient to ensure the inclusion of a condition in the enabling Act which required operational running on the branch lines before the route to Southend was opened.

Within three years of parliamentary approval being granted the necessary land had been acquired and construction had begun, Walter Scott & Co. of Newcastle being awarded the £411, 858 13s. 6d. contract for the construction of the new lines and stations. This figure does not include land acquisition costs which, if one Woodham example is any guide, would have been considerable: the Drapers' Company extracted from the railway company in excess of £1,000 for three acres of land needed for the line at Saltcoats Farm when normal agricultural land values were below £10 per acre. Obviously the land-owners' support for the line did not extend to granting advantageous land deals to the railway company.

If the branch lines to Maldon and Southminster had in any way been seen as a sop this certainly was not apparent in the level of trackside infrastructure. The junction at Woodham, was a particularly impressive facility with platforms, footbridge, waiting rooms, coalyard, cattle pens, turntable and workers' cottages. It was perhaps typical of Victorian enterprise and vision to make provision on this scale in the middle of what, after all, was still a thinly populated agricultural area.

The line to Southminster opened for goods traffic on Saturday 1 June 1889. The line's first train, 'a very respectable locomotive with cattle trucks and everything complete' according to a contemporary newspaper account,[2] arrived at the end of the line one hour and 20 minutes late: an inauspicious start to a service that so drastically altered the face of Woodham in succeeding years.

The passenger service began one month later on Monday 1 July 1889. By this time the station at Woodham, which at first had been called Woodham Fen, had been renamed Woodham Ferris following representations from residents in the neighbourhood. The explanation for the request was that it was claimed that there was no such place as Woodham Fen near the station, which is odd considering that the nearby Woodham Fen had been marked on maps as such for some time whilst the village 'Woodham Ferris' was one mile to the north. The station stoically omits the 'South' in its name to this day.

Initially there were six trains each way. The fastest through trains were timetabled to reach London's Liverpool Street in one hour 20 minutes from Woodham and the advertised return fare was 2s. 6d. (12½ pence).

So far as the Southminster line was concerned the staggered opening requirements of the 1883 Act were met; the Wickford to Southend line opened three months later at which time the Maldon branch also became operational. The story of the Woodham to Maldon line is a relatively short one. The passenger service lasted just 50 years, ceasing in 1939 and freight services were withdrawn in 1953. The sister line to Southminster survived and its fortunes have mirrored those of the national network; diesel passenger trains replaced steam in 1956, drastic rationalisation occurred in 1968 and electrification, with the restoration of some through journeys to Liverpool Street, was completed in 1986.

18. Standing with his faithful assistant Patch on the Southminster branch line is Robert 'Dick' Clark who was a resident ganger at Woodham Ferrers from 1889 to 1919. The railway cottages and the Maldon branch line lie behind him.

19. Patiently posing for the photographer in their white pinafore dresses, these girls are standing in front of the three pairs of cottages built for railway workers. The cottages were built to a standard branch-line pattern by the main contractor for the line, Walter Scott & Co. The price for all six cottages was £1,919 15s. 2d.

20. This view from the 1920s
emphasises the slight cutting that
the railway runs in at the level
crossing. Before the First World
War the gatekeeper supplemented
his G.E.R. income by providing
additional services to the
embryonic community: he mended
shoes and provided a boys'
hairdressing service in his hut by
the gates.

21. Members of the Neale and
Clark families stand outside
5 Railway Cottages in August
1910. Belonging to a Great Eastern
Railway family seems to have been
a serious business.

22. The clutter on the platforms, seen here in the 1940s, includes, on the extreme left, baskets for mushrooms or fruit. These are a reminder of the station's primary function as a centre for gathering and transporting horticultural produce bound for London's markets from the surrounding farms and nurseries.

23. It seems that the main approach to the station buildings on the northern side of the line was rarely photographed. This picture shows part of the range of buildings, with the stationmaster's house and the station entrance, now demolished, beyond.

24. In this 1911 view of Woodham Ferrers junction the cattle pens and loading bay can be seen on the left and the turntable, by this time disused, on the right. It was an impressive junction to establish in what was, in the 1880s, an area of farmland one mile from the nearest village.

25. A Fred Spalding photograph, with his characteristic ever-circling birds painted into an otherwise featureless sky. It shows a Class E10 locomotive standing in the station with a five-coach train in about 1904.

26. A Class B12 (4-6-0) locomotive hauls a train out of Woodham Ferrers station on the last day of passenger steam service on the branch line to Southminster on 16 September 1956. Steam locomotives were to be seen on the line for another five years hauling goods or maintenance trains.

27. The train and station staff: (left to right) Warwick Bridge, Charlie Potter, Arthur Clark and Arthur Algar, the stationmaster, stand on the platform on that sunny September day which marked the end of passenger steam train service on the branch line.

28. The evening sun is casting long shadows across the platform, but does little to brighten up a somewhat grubby ex-Great Eastern J17 locomotive waiting with an 'up' goods train in August 1959.

29. A picture which epitomises the change-over period in the station's history. The motive power reflects the modern era but, for the time being, the infrastructure of the steam era is still prevalent, although the loading bay on the right is now looking rather overgrown.

30. Almost four years after the withdrawal of steam-hauled passenger trains a Great Eastern J20 (0-6-0) locomotive pauses at Woodham Ferrers for the photograph that records the last steam hauled goods train on the branch line. The date is 26 August 1960.

31.   The tender of the last steam locomotive to work on the branch line provided the viewpoint for this picture of the station and its rural surroundings in August 1961. The locomotive, a Class B1 (4-6-0), is waiting in a siding with a short ballast train.

BRITISH TRANSPORT COMMISSION

EASTERN REGION
GREAT EASTERN LINE

COMPETITION FOR
BEST KEPT STATIONS
1961

FIRST CLASS
PRIZE

awarded to *Woodham Ferrers* Station

_____ W.S. Thorne _____ Line Traffic Manager
                            (Great Eastern)

32. In its heyday Woodham Ferrers station was a frequent recipient of Best Kept Station certificates. The framed certificates survived in the ticket office long after their surroundings ceased to deserve them.

33.   Well into the diesel era the station was well maintained, as this photograph from the mid-1960s shows. The footbridge roof is in the process of being replaced and the original station lamps are still in position. This three-car diesel is bound for Southminster, having just passed the goods yard where a wagon is visible in the background.

34.   5 April 1963 was a significant date in the history of the surviving Southminster branch line. This special 'double-headed' train at Woodham Ferrers station is returning guests to London who had earlier attended the opening ceremony of the nuclear power station at Bradwell. The transport of nuclear waste by rail was undoubtedly a significant reason for the survival of the line.

35.   At its peak Woodham Ferrers junction contained 17 sets of points. With lines reduced to a single track in 1968 the final sets were removed, and with them the signal box. With demolition men about to move in, the photographer gives us a final view of the deserted signal box, from where the junction had been kept running smoothly for almost 80 years.

36. A 1968 picture of the station taken from the south side of the line near the site of the former turntable, showing the buildings that were demolished later that year.

37. Looking west from the doomed footbridge in 1968 the alignments of some of the lifted tracks can still be seen. The small building, centre right, is the old weighbridge hut, whilst beyond, the former goodsyard accommodates a coalyard.

The railway, as hoped, did provide a welcome stimulus for agriculture in the area. Up until this time sailing barges were the best means of bulk transport and it is ironic that this bulk transport in the 1880s included much of the material for the construction of the new line which hastened the demise of the waterborne trade.

In respect of navigable waterways, Woodham enjoyed an advantageous position. Its river frontage and two creeks are the farthest inland stretches of tidal water in Essex with the single exception of the highest navigable point of the River Crouch upstream at Battlesbridge. It is an advantage that has remained and has been extolled for centuries. In 1582 the manorial survey had highlighted the proximity of the nearby tidal waters and the ease of transport to London and a mid-19th century sales brochure for Champions Farm slightly stretched a point to claim that the farm 'extends to the River and commands the advantages of the Great Wharfs at Hulbridge for obtaining manures of all kinds, and for shipping its produce to London'.[3]

38. The view east from the footbridge in 1968 shows the route of the Maldon branch directly ahead. By now, some eight years after the branch line had been removed, the embankment is considerably overgrown.

Prior to the arrival of the railway the alternative means of transporting materials was by road, a method that could never have been easy over the heavy clay soils of southern Essex. As if to emphasise the particular difficulties faced by road travellers in this part of the county, the neighbouring parish of Rettendon on the London side of Woodham is said to derive its name from a corruption of two Saxon words which mean 'sad riding' on account of its bad roads.

Whilst early road travellers may have been subjected to much hardship, they at least apparently had the local advantage of a bridge over the River Crouch between Woodham and Hullbridge; a trip that today entails a detour of some six miles. Evidence for the existence of such a bridge can not only be found on some early maps but also in a number of presentments in the Essex Quarter Sessions records. The demise of the bridge occurred some time in the 17th century and thereafter references to the Hullbridge crossing are predominantly in relation to ferries or ferrymen and their extortionate fares.

1.   The Proposed Railway from Wickford to Southminster, *Essex County Chronicle*, 30 March 1883.
2.   The Dengie Hundred Railway, *Essex County Chronicle*, 7 June 1889.
3.   *Champions Farm*, sale catalogue (1854). E.R.O. D/Dop, B82.

LL BRIDGE . 1797

Fred Spalding Photo. Chelmsford. Copyright

39.   The Hullbridge side of the river opposite South Woodham Ferrers is one of the few areas of the River Crouch where there is a natural bank rather than a sea wall. Consequently the village extended to the water's edge and a number of jetties were built along this stretch of the river. This view dates from the early 1900s.

40. Herbert Lazell (centre) directs his team of workers in the 1920s in the never-ending efforts to keep South Woodham's sea wall up to the required standard. The rather shallow wheelbarrows seen here were used because of the very heavy clay that was being carried.

41. With waters navigable by sailing barges on three sides of South Woodham, there were a number of sites at which vessels could be moored for loading and unloading. The southern end of Hullbridge Road was obviously a convenient point, and it was from here, for example, that stones for road maintenance in the area were unloaded.

42. The tide is beginning to ebb in this inter-war view, as the ferryman rows his passengers towards the South Woodham Ferrers bank. At high tide the water crossing was more than three times the low tide equivalent.

43. This view in about 1923 shows the well defined causeways which led down to the ford.

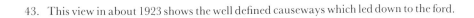

44. Dick Hymas, pictured here, was the last ferryman to provide a regular ferry service across the river between South Woodham Ferrers and Hullbridge, a role he fulfilled for more than 20 years. He ceased operations in 1948, thus bringing to an end a service which can be traced back at least 300 years.

45. A tranquil riverside scene in 1924 with some 25 children on the South Woodham Ferrers side awaiting the arrival of their school transport. Perhaps the presence of at least three adults in the group reflects the concern that parents had over the hazards of the river crossing, where two men had been drowned in the previous year.

46.   The winter of 1962-3 saw heavy snow and freezing conditions turn the River Crouch at South Woodham Ferrers into a picturesque ice floe, repeating the conditions and scenes last experienced in the area in 1928.

47.   The disadvantages of locating a weekend retreat too close to the tidal waters around South Woodham Ferrers were evident on more than one occasion in the inter-war years. This is the Fenn Creek area in 1938.

48. The low-lying land adjacent to Fenn Brook has been vulnerable to flooding, not only from high tides as in 1953, but also during times of heavy rainfall as here in the early 1960s.

49. The bow wave from a passing lorry washes into a doorway of *The Whalebone* whilst pedestrians contemplate the obstacle.

50. Why walk on the verge when there is a perfectly good flooded road to struggle through?

51.   This old gated bridge once carried the main access track as it crossed Fenn Creek to Eyotts Farm. An unsubstantiated local story is that during the Napoleonic Wars, when the nearby Danbury Common was used as an army camp ground, this bridge was built by prisoners of war.

Plotland Development

In the decade after the opening of the railway, Woodham became part of a dramatic development process, sometimes called plotland development, which was to have far reaching effects over vast tracts of south-east Essex. The process was prompted by the virtual collapse of the farming industry on the heavy London clay soils of this part of Essex and the simultaneous provision of a rail network in the area. The subdivision and sale for development of uneconomic agricultural land in areas served by the new railway stations fulfilled the aims of railway companies and landowners alike. Both groups were looking for a return on their investment which the development of plotlands and the expansion of population appeared to promise.

In the South Woodham Ferrers area the process began in 1893 when the 538-acre Champions Farm, then a struggling agricultural unit, was auctioned with a reserve price of just £4,500. It was purchased by a certain Henry Jesty Ellis Brake, an estate agent and surveyor from Farnborough, Hampshire. The Brake family firm, operating as Brake and Son and Brake Estates, were specialists in plotland development. Their operation at South Woodham Ferrers, on what they called the Champions Hall Estate, was aimed at 'City Men, Market Gardeners, Fruit and Flower Growers and Others requiring Good Cheap Land' together with 'those with small means who are desirous to live a retired country life'. The sales literature proclaimed that 'the Estate has been conveniently laid out in plots to suit all purchasers ...', the one-acre plots at the rate of £20 each and individual building plots with frontages to Hullbridge Road and new estate roads from £10 each.[1] At a time when an agricultural labourer might expect to earn 15s. (75 pence) a week this land was comparatively cheap.

52. One of the thousands of receipts issued to South Woodham Ferrers plot purchasers. Repayments at a few shillings a month must have presented H. W. Brake's administrative machinery with a considerable challenge.

EYOTTS ESTATE, WOODHAM FERRIS,

ESSEX.

Particulars, Plan, and Conditions of Sale of about

200 Plots of Freehold Building Land

VIEW OF RESIDENCE TO BE OFFERED AT THIS SALE.

Which will be Sold on the Estate,

On TUESDAY, AUGUST 1st, 1899, at 2 p.m.

FREE LUNCHEON WILL BE PROVIDED AT 1 p.m.   A limited number of Railway Tickets will be issued at 2/- each, returnable to Purchasers.

These Tickets will be available by the Special Train leaving Liverpool Street at 10.50 a.m., calling at Stratford.

Solicitors—Messrs POWELL & ROGERS,
17, Essex Street, Strand, W.C.

Auctioneers—Messrs PROTHEROE & MORRIS,
67 & 68, Cheapside, London, E.C.

A 146

53.   This sales catalogue for plots on part of the Eyotts Estate was produced for the auction held at the estate on 1 August 1899.

54. In about 1923 Frank Buxton, having moved from Deptford to lodgings in Woodham Ferrers, built his first home in South Woodham Ferrers. Here he stands outside his recently completed handiwork, Shardeloes, on the western side of Elm Road on the Champions Estate.

55. Unlike the Eyotts Estate, where land was auctioned, plots on the Champions Estate were sold at a fixed price. Individual building plots were available in Sections A to H fronting the main roads. Elsewhere on the estate, plots with a minimum size of one acre were offered for sale.

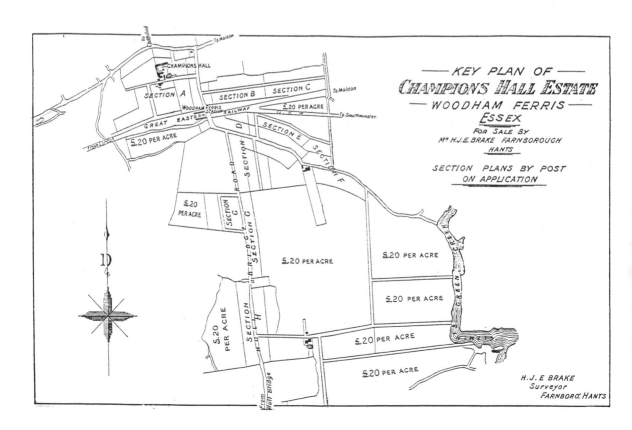

The neighbouring Eyotts Farm soon followed the example set by its larger neighbour and between 1899 and 1901 special train excursions, at a return fare of 2s. (10 pence) returnable to plot purchasers, conveyed hundreds of potential buyers from London to free luncheons at Stratford and to auction sales on the Eyotts Estate. The plots were auctioned for the owner, Joseph Rettallack-Maloney a land surveyor, by auctioneers Protheroe and Morris of Cheapside, London. The sales brochure praised the virtues of the estate which 'occupies exceedingly fine views of the surrounding country and River Scenery, and slopes gently down to the river rendering plots now offered very desirable for the creation of Country residences, bungalows and villas'.[2]

Although the estate owners provided no made-up roads nor services, which resulted in some plot purchasers having to make a two-mile round trip for water supplies, the sales on the Eyotts Estate were at least the subject of a comprehensive list of building and land use conditions. For example, houses were not to be of less value than £150 for each house or £250 per pair, houses were to be built facing the road and set back at least 20 ft. from the plot frontage and no caravans, huts or houses on wheels were to be allowed. Whether there ever was the intention to enforce these sales conditions or whether they constituted part of the dream that was being sold to Londoners must be open to debate.

Gradually as sales were completed, newcomers started to arrive in the area and a haphazard development began to take place. Such newcomers were not always welcomed and as early as 1898 there was considerable local concern about the quality of dwellings that were being built on the plotland estates. Newcomers were described as squatters whose style of living 'might do in the Australian bush or the American backwoods but it is hardly what one might expect in the highly civilised county of Essex'.[3]

56. Building plots in Fairview Road, seen here in 1972, on the south-facing slopes overlooking Fenn Creek, found ready purchasers in the early estate auctions. They became popular for holiday and weekend cottages and less so for smallholdings, being at the outer extremes of an uncertain road system.

57. The Beavins family were typical of a number of London families who lovingly constructed their weekend cottage from whatever materials came to hand. This part of their countryside retreat, River View, pictured here in the 1930s, housed kitchen, living and sleeping accommodation.

58. Nearby on their plot which lay beside Fenn Creek, this small hut, complete with rudimentary drainage system, provided additional sleeping space for family and friends.

59.   The name, River View, remained the same into the 1970s, but the building was no longer recognisable as either of those which had first appeared on the site over 40 years earlier.

60. South Woodham Ferrers was a place for taking holidays. St Mary's church is a Woodham Ferrers interloper in this collection of inter-war views of South Woodham Ferrers. The central roundel features Shaw Farm.

61. An atmospheric view of the creekside huts, with timber access ways across drainage ditches.

62. In 1889 the Eyotts Estate auctioneers had sold the ditch-dissected meadow along a 300-yard length of Fenn Creek as a single plot. It was subsequently developed with buildings almost of beach-hut size and quality, all of which have been demolished.

63. This property, Fennhaven, was the base for the operations of Country Homes Limited in the 1920s.

64. Marie Dean, at the western end of York Road (see 72), was typical of the timber and asbestos properties built by Country Homes Ltd. Despite the company's apparent reluctance to comply with building bye-laws in force in the 1920s, some of their products lasted to provide permanent homes into the 1970s.

65. Sans Jean, in The Drive, was another of the properties of Country Homes Ltd. Known locally as 'The Asbestos Kings', because of their extensive use of asbestos, the company built about twenty such cottages in the area from the mid-1920s onwards.

66. The Eyotts sale
stipulation that no plot
should be used for sheds,
huts nor properties of less
value than £150 does not
appear to have been
enforced. This building
occupied plot 999 at the
western end of York Road
until the early 1970s.

67. During the inter-war
years in particular, the
plotland estates presented
an ever-changing scene of
small-scale building works,
fencing operations, and not a
few boundary disputes. This
1920s view of the western
end of Victoria Road near
Fenn Creek shows evidence
of recent fencing work on
Ministry-owned land on the
right.

Of more significance than the immediate impact of the new buildings and their occupants however was the radically different pattern of land division and land ownership that had emerged in the span of a few years. A rectilinear network of unmade tracks now gave access to land divided into scattered plots being developed by their new owners. Problems were not confined to jibes from established Essex residents; there were numerous boundary disputes and within a few years of development commencing, Chelmsford Rural District Council had summonsed several occupiers for failing to comply with bye-laws and the Public Health Acts. One case involving Horace Adolphus Mudd made national headlines when an unpaid fine for contravening bye-laws led to a seven-day prison sentence. Some purchasers were simply unable to build a property of reasonable standards whilst keeping up their purchase money repayments.

A further factor militating against the success of these plotland schemes was that the supply of land bore little relation to public demand. South Woodham Ferrers found itself competing for business with a multiplicity of similar rival schemes in south Essex and north Kent. On the Champions and Eyotts estates alone more than 700 acres of land, divided into more than 2,000 plots, had been offered for sale in the decade following 1895. However this represented probably less than two per cent of the total amount of land offered for building plots in south Essex in this period. It is not surprising therefore that, although land was relatively cheap, the development of sites in South Woodham Ferrers was sporadic and the vast majority of plots remained unsold or undeveloped before the First World War. In 1915 Rettallack-Maloney sold his remaining considerable interests on the Eyotts Estate to an entrepreneurial insurance broker Thomas Cowper, and the Brakes were still selling land on the Champions Estate 30 years after the original sales had taken place.

Despite these uncertain beginnings, in the period prior to the Great War the area could boast a number of small shops, an hotel, post office and two churches: a Congregational chapel opened in 1903 and St Mary's Mission Hall was established in 1904. To house the newcomers, buildings of great variety were being erected, ranging from shacks of wood, asbestos and corrugated iron for weekend or holiday use to soundly built brick houses and bungalows. Bricks produced from the local clay were available from the works of the Woodham Ferris Brick Company which traded under the name A. Blake after 1902. The firm soon became the area's largest single employer and operated between 1898 and about 1908 from a site on the eastern edge of the Champions Estate where it had its own landing stage at Clementsgreen Creek.

Such have been the radical changes brought about by the construction of the new town in recent years that it is often difficult to pinpoint the sites of particular properties, or to envisage how parts of the town area would have once appeared. It is possible, however, to find vegetation, boundaries and ponds which have survived and which help to identify parts of the former plotland layout. In the following pages maps of parts of the present-day town are shown alongside the equivalent area in 1972, and from these some of the surviving features can be identified. The sites of the properties illustrated are indicated on the modern map in each case. An overall map which shows the locations of these extracts can be found on the end papers of this book.

1. *Champions Hall Estate*, sales catalogue, *c*.1910. E.R.O. B5217.
2. *Eyotts Estate*, sales catalogue, (1899). E.R.O. A146.
3. Squatters at Woodham, *The Essex Weekly News*, 25 March 1898.

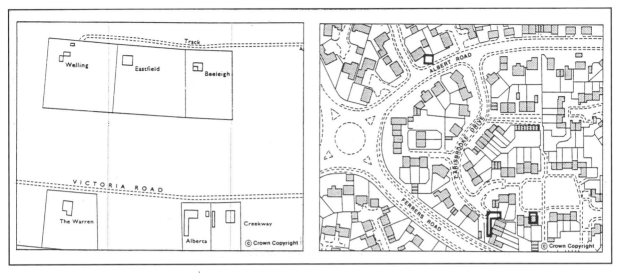

68. Area 1. Illustrating a 'clean sheet' approach to housing layout, very little remains on the ground to relate the 1972 layout and the present-day development. However, the plans do illustrate the point that the new layout made a more economic use of land for housing purposes: six dwellings within the mapped area have been replaced by more than a hundred.

69. A new roof, new flooring, main drainage and central heating had gradually transformed the timber-framed Creekway into comfortable permanent living accommodation by the early 1970s. The property was then acquired for development and was demolished.

70. The timber-framed bungalow, Alberta, which was formerly known more romantically as Moonlight Villa, shared its quarter-acre site with a range of kennels and runs for dogs. A plotland environment was particularly suitable for those who, for various reasons, required a degree of isolation.

71. Planning policies militated against the development of isolated sites in the plotland area. The site at Eastfield was an exception, and subject to constructing a 200-yard section of new road the owner was granted permission to build a new bungalow. The original bungalow was becoming dilapidated by 1972, but the project to replace it never came to fruition.

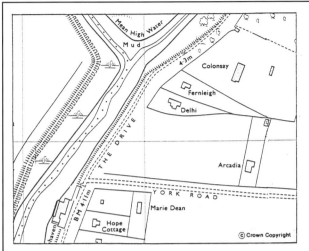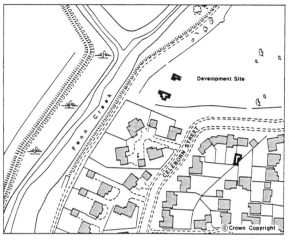

72. Area 2. In addition to the properties shown here and indicated on the present-day map, some of the cottages built by Country Homes Ltd. were in this area (see illustrations 64 and 65).

73. Delhi occupied one of the popular creekside locations on the Eyotts Estate. Consideration was given to excluding these sites from the new town area, but after doing so Essex County Council concluded that comprehensive development should extend to the edge of the creek.

74. Ownership of lengths of creek frontage was transferred by Country Homes Ltd. to purchasers of plots in The Drive. This gave properties such as Fernleigh, the advantages of mooring space beside the creek. The waters were navigable for Thames sailing barges up to this point.

75. Arcadia in York Road was built on plots 403 and 404 on the Eyotts Estate. The site was virtually surrounded by land acquired under emergency procedures in the Great War, and still retained by the Ministry of Agriculture in 1972.

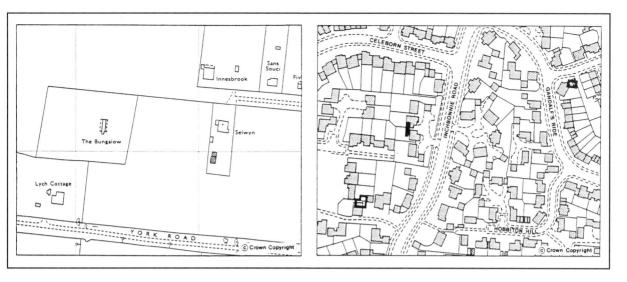

76. Area 3. Comparison of these maps will reveal that a number of hedgerows around plot boundaries and along estate roads have been retained in today's development, particularly around The Bungalow and Selwyn.

77. The Bungalow was one of a number of railway carriages used as living or holiday accommodation in the area until the early 1970s. This one is an ex-Great Eastern Railway six-wheeler second-class carriage of 1906.

78. Lych Cottage in York Road demonstrates the signs of incremental growth and do-it-yourself improvements typical of many properties on plotland estates.

79. Although the Eyotts Estate had been divided into building plots of 20-ft. width, local bye-laws did not permit the construction of a timber building in such a constricted space. Sans Souci, for example, was built on three plots, nos. 269-271: a more realistic minimum size for a small dwelling.

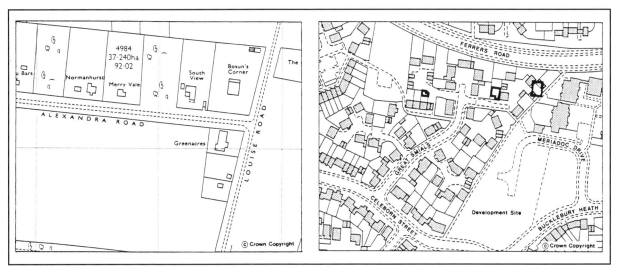

80. Area 4. On the northern edge of their housing site, developers Countryside Properties adopted the site of Normanhurst, formerly five plots on the Eyotts Estate, as a ready-made hedge-lined play area on their Ayotts Hurst estate. Elsewhere, the substantial hedge on the northern edge of the Alexandra Road properties is retained adjacent to Ferrers Road.

81. It appears to have been a minority of plots that were developed by the first purchasers at the turn of the century; inter-war years in particular were characterised by numerous speculative land deals. South View, for example, was built in the late 1920s only after its site had passed through the hands of four separate owners.

82.　Bosun's Corner stood on a plot originally sold by auction in 1902 and was a brick-built four-bedroomed bungalow formerly known as Ozokozy.

83.　Although it was subject to the same haphazard influences that produced random groupings of buildings elsewhere, Alexandra Road attracted a particular type of building which caused the road to be referred to locally as Rabbit Hutch Lane. The building in this picture is called Merryvale.

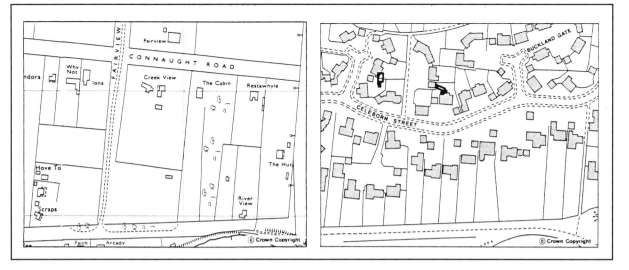

84. Area 5. The present-day housing layout on the south facing slope near Fenn Creek bears a marked similarity with that which it replaced. Even the method of development in this instance, by the release of individual building plots for 'self build' owners, mirrored that of almost a century earlier.

85. Iona in Connaught Road was typical of a number of smaller, well maintained properties on the Eyotts Estate, its neat veranda a typical feature of inter-war buildings of this type.

86. With fewer rules governing such matters than in today's town, home extension and improvement was sometimes more a way of life than a hobby on the plotland estates. The building materials in evidence at Creek View show that such activity continued into the 1970s even as the new town proposals were being formulated.

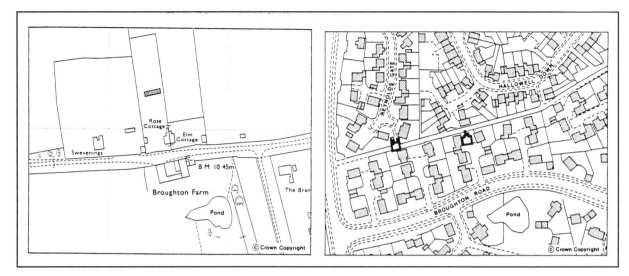

87. Area 6. The pond and wooded area shown on the 1972 map have been retained to good effect in the modern development. The sites on the present-day map were developed between 1982 and 1986.

88. Described in the 1893 sale of Champions Farm as '2 recently built brick and slated cottages each containing six rooms', Elm Cottage and Rose Cottage were acquired by Henry Brake when he purchased the farm. In 1899 they were sold as part of his land sales.

89. Swevenings had been the location of another of South Woodham's poultry farms. The grounds originally formed part of the seven-acre landholding of the Gittins family, whose brickworks were established nearby. Two ponds from these brickworks survive on the Littlecroft development which is to the north-east of the area shown on the map.

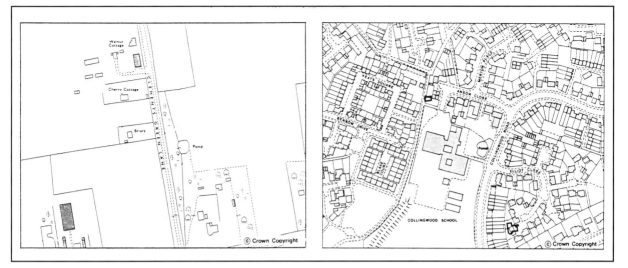

© Crown Copyright   © Crown Copyright

90.   Area 7. Unlike a number of other ponds in the vicinity, the pond retained in today's development did not derive from brick-making activities, but existed within a field boundary on Champions Farm many years before the subdivision of the land for building purposes.

91.   Although properties on this part of the Champions Estate were generally permanent homes of a reasonable size, there were exceptions. Cherry Cottage was one such building in Clements Green Lane.

92.   In a plotland environment it soon becomes an overworked phrase to describe buildings as incongruous, but The Gables (unnamed on the 1972 map), with its elegant tiled roof, would surely be more appropriate in a leafy suburb than surrounded by scrub half a mile from the nearest surfaced road.

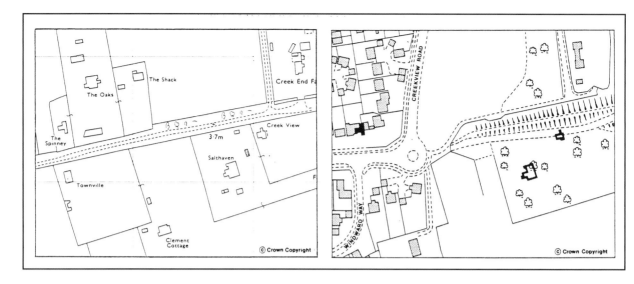

93.   Area 8. An important element in the plan for the new town was the area of open space between the new development and the surrounding tidal waters. Therefore some properties seen on the 1972 map were acquired and demolished, but their sites remain undeveloped.

94.   The mature oak tree on the Top Barn Lane frontage of The Spinney now occupies a prominent place in today's Broughton Road.

95. In exceptional weather and tide conditions, buildings on the low-lying land close to the seawall were liable to suffer flooding. The property at Creek View demonstrated a solution to this problem, which at the same time provided improved views over the seawall.

96. Although standing more than 100 yards from Clementsgreen Creek, the L-shaped site of Salthaven extended round the edge of the adjoining orchard to the mean high water mark of the creek.

Education and Community Life

97. The Smallholders' Hall, erected under the auspices of the South Woodham Smallholders and Social Society Ltd., was opened in February 1929. Share capital at five shillings each share was raised towards its £1,600 cost, and it represented a remarkable collective achievement by local people. The present village hall replaced the original hall in 1973.

98. One of the five shilling shares of the Society, issued to local trader George Mudford in 1927.

Certificate No. 157   No. of Shares 1

South Woodham Smallholders and Social Society,

LIMITED.   Regd. No. 9726 R Essex.

(Registered under the Industrial and Provident Societies Act. 1893).

This is to Certify *that George Mudford*

of Hullbridge Road South Woodham

is the Proprietor of *One* Fully paid Five Shilling Shares

numbered *546* to *—* inclusive, in the above-named

Society, subject to that Society's Registered Rules.

Given under the Seal of The South Woodham Smallholders and Social

Society, Limited, this *8th* day of *July* 192*7*

Eric D Priest
Samuel Lewin   } Members of Committee of Management.

R Harrington Secretary.

NOTE.—No transfer of any portion of the Shares can be made except on the form prescribed and lodged with the Secretary.

99.   During the Second World War the village had its own part-time fire service, which operated from a private house on the Burnham Road near the eastern end of King Edward's Road. The village suffered comparatively light damage in the war, although unfortunately there was one fatality when a bomb fell in Albert Road.

100.   During the Second World War the hall fulfilled a purpose which even the visionaries behind its construction could hardly have foreseen. As a small contribution to the country's wartime emergency plans it was designated as an emergency hospital. In this 1940 view, Woodham Ferrers hospital supply members are arriving at the hall for their annual meeting.

101. *The Whalebone*, the origins of which can be traced back for more than two centuries, was popular with train travellers before the *Railway Hotel* was built. From the front of the building hung a piece of whalebone, but there is nothing positive to relate this to the whale reported as meeting its end in the River Crouch in 1768.

102. The building was the subject of much needed restoration in the early years of this century. Early one morning in November 1905, however, a fire completely destroyed the newly restored building despite the efforts of the landlord, local constables and farmworkers.

103. Whilst business continued in a stable which survived the fire, Gravesend Brewery, the owner of the building, constructed a new building on the site. The identities of this group posing in front of the property in its original rebuilt form are unknown.

104. By the early 1920s the building had been half rendered, and began to appear closer to its present-day, extended form. Staff and customers wait for the photographer to complete his work.

105. An early view of the *Railway Hotel*. Its name-board advertises 'Accommodation of visitors, sportsmen, cyclists and others, good stabling for horses, boxes for hunters, traps for hire'. It is worth extending the picture beyond the frame of the photographer's trim-line to include the horse and carriage standing in the shadows outside the post office building.

106. In 1904 the tiny St Mary's Mission Hall was established in Hullbridge Road to serve South Woodham's newcomers, its parent church being St Mary's in Woodham Ferrers. The roof of the building in this 1940 photograph shows evidence of the extension added some eight years earlier.

107.   The third place of worship to be built in the growing village was the Baptist church, seen here under construction in Clements Green Lane. The building was constructed using voluntary labour and opened in 1926. The extensive use of timber and corrugated iron is typical of many of the early buildings in the area.

108.   A small crowd dressed in their Sunday best gather to witness the opening ceremony of the church on Whit Monday in 1926. The building, although much altered, survives today and is still used for Christian worship.

BAPTIST CHURCH,

SOUTH WOODHAM FERRERS,

Will (D.V.) be

OPENED

On

Whit Monday, May 24th, 1926,

At 3.15 p.m.

A SERMON will be PREACHED by

PASTOR T. REYNOLDS,

Of ST. JOHN'S WOOD, at 3.30 p.m.

TEA at 5.15 p.m.   Tickets, Sixpence each.

A PUBLIC MEETING

Will be held in the Evening.   Chair to be taken at 7 o'clock.

Addresses by Pastor T. Reynolds

And others.

A COLLECTION WILL BE TAKEN.

Dilliway & Co., Printers, Burnham.

109. A handbill advertised the opening of the Baptist church with tickets available at 6d. each.

110. The independent Assembly Mission Hall in Hullbridge Road opened in May 1931. Local builders, the Deavin family, were prime movers in the project. In 1945 the Friends' Evangelistic Band assumed responsibility for the church and Christian witness on the same site continues in the Evangelical church today.

111. One cannot help thinking that members of the Rayleigh Men's Own Brass Band must have accounted for half the space in the small hall when they assembled for the advertised Musical Evening in 1936.

112. South Woodham's fifth church, which opened in 1932, was another Baptist church and is the nearer of the two buildings in this view from 1940. The building became part of the adjoining school premises in 1954.

113. The Deavin children set out from their Hullbridge Road home on their way to the river crossing and to school. The poor condition of the road is evident in this view from about 1907.

114. In 1924, five years before South Woodham Ferrers gained its own school, schoolchildren are seen here alighting from the cart that has brought them across the river and, with varying degrees of enthusiasm, heading off for Hullbridge school.

115. A crowded boat returns South Woodham Ferrers children from school at high tide with what appears to be at least one more boatload of pupils waiting their turn on the Hullbridge side.

116. Woodham Ferrers school in the neighbouring village catered for the small number of children who did not attend school in Hullbridge; generally these were from families that lived north of the railway line. Fidgeting in the front row in this 1914 school photograph is Gerty Clark from South Woodham (fifth from left).

117. The one mile walk to Woodham Ferrers school, although arduous, was not the hazardous journey that might be imagined today; a fact amply demonstrated by this view of an aged couple casually descending Happy Valley between the two villages.

118. The Women's Institute hall, pictured here in 1940, was opened in 1927, three years after the formation of the South Woodham Ferrers branch of the Women's Institute. The hall served an additional purpose as the village's Catholic church in the 1950s and 1960s.

Inter-War Years

Although the initial take up of land on the Champions and Eyotts estates had been relatively slow, the 1920s were to witness an upsurge in interest in the area. With a continuing supply of cheap land, the growing village (which had been formally labelled as South Woodham Ferrers in 1913) entered a dynamic building period as more and more of the plots were sold and developed. Where land had been acquired of sufficient size, nurseries and smallholdings became established and poultry farming in particular began to flourish. The advantage of poultry farming to the plot owner was the quick financial return that it could bring and at its peak in the early 1930s it has been estimated that there were some 20,000 free-range chickens in and around the village. However the open runs were gradually killing off the land and, as national trends swung towards more intensive methods, the essentially small-scale concerns in South Woodham Ferrers were not in a position to adapt and by the Second World War poultry farming in the area had almost disappeared.

The situation that had developed by the early 1920s, of a large number of landowners attempting to make a living from the land, led in 1923 to the formation of the South Woodham Smallholders and Social Society, the membership of which numbered 137 at the end of its first year of operation. The objectives of this society were to minimise local competition, to provide advantages of bulk buying for local smallholders and to build a hall in the village for trading and social recreation. This latter objective was realised in 1929 when the South Woodham Smallholders Hall, later called the village hall, was opened near the northern end of Hullbridge Road. It stood for 44 years as a symbol of the co-operative spirit that existed in the growing village in the 1920s.

1929 also saw the opening of South Woodham's long-awaited first school which was built in Hullbridge Road. For some years parents had been concerned about the hazards of the daily river crossing to the school in Hullbridge and lobbied for a school to be built in South Woodham Ferrers. This concern had intensified when Mr. T. Deeks, licensee of *The Whalebone* and Sydney Osborne, a labourer, had been drowned at the ford in 1923. The school was opened by the headmistress, Kathleen Foulgar, with 57 pupils on the roll on the first day.

Another project which reached fruition at the end of the 1920s was the building of the Women's Institute Hall. The Women's Institute had started in South Woodham Ferrers in 1924 and originally met in St Mary's Mission Hall.

The spiritual needs of the village's residents were being met by an increasing number of churches. A Baptist church opened in Clements Green Lane in 1926; the Assembly Mission Hall, later to be called the Evangelical Church, opened in 1931 followed shortly afterwards by a second Baptist church. This last named building was erected on a site next to the school and in 1954 was incorporated into the school premises where it remained into the 1990s.

Business opportunities increased as the population grew and, apart from a growing number of shops, such as those of the Davisons, the village gained Mudford's haulage business and, on the northern edge of its area, South Woodham Garage.

119. At the corner of The Chase a 60-ft. length of an ex-army hut became a general store. It was purchased from the nearby camp at Danbury Park for £100 after the First World War.

Not all residents in the area were occupiers of self-built properties. By the 1920s new forces were at work. The village's first four council houses were built on the northern edge of the village on land that had not formed part of either of the two plotland estates and other ready-built homes were being provided by Country Homes Ltd. This company operated in several plotland areas in south Essex and built a number of timber and asbestos premises on both the Champions and Eyotts estates, using a small hut near the station as their estate office. The company's efforts did not meet with universal approval, however, and in 1924 it was summonsed for contravening a number of building bye-laws. In defence it was claimed that the houses were simply intended for weekend Londoners and cost about £150 each.

Others wanting ready-made but rather less orthodox premises could purchase redundant railway carriages and about a dozen of these found their way to sites in the village. Seven survived into the 1970s including a pair of rare 1893 family saloon carriages originally built for private hire by single families and linked to form a single dwelling on the Eyotts Estate.

In parallel with these developments, services associated with 20th-century civilisation began to reach South Woodham Ferrers: metalled roads and telephones by the mid-1920s and electricity within another decade, although the village had to wait until 1966 for main drainage. Not all plot dwellers appreciated these civilising intrusions.

Shops and Businesses

120.   Red Cottage Stores was one of the first shops in the village. It resulted from a conversion of part of the range of old cottages at William Tabrum's Copyhold near the junction of today's Wickford Road and Hullbridge Road.

121.   The Davison family had a number of commercial interests in the growing village. Here Albert Davison stands at their second shop immediately south of the level crossing in Hullbridge Road. The newspaper placards show that the photograph was taken in the summer of 1927.

122.   The post office in South Woodham Ferrers was one of the first buildings erected after the railway opened. It was built adjacent to the vacant site reserved for the *Railway Hotel* and served the village until the early 1930s, when the post office business transferred to Davison's Stores near The Chase. The building itself survived into the 1990s.

123.   Davison's Stores in Hullbridge Road near The Chase was a general store established after the First World War. In 1933 the store had taken over the role of post office in the village, and whilst still stocking the ubiquitous chicken wire had further widened its advertised range of goods to include cycle accessories.

124.   The post office continued its migration between properties in this stretch of Hullbridge Road after the Second World War, when business transferred from Davison's to its present site. Business continued much as before, as this view shows, until the site was developed for housing.

125. Orchard Stores was known as Cash Stores from about 1903, and traded under the name F. W. Deavin who built the property. The Deavins were one of the most prolific and respected of local builders, whose work stood in stark contrast to some of the temporary structures being erected. This building survives as a private house near today's Pintolls.

126. A rare survivor from pre-railway Woodham was this pair of timber cottages in Hullbridge Road at the north-eastern extremity of the Eyotts Farm landholding. Percy Stores occupies the converted northern end of the premises in this inter-war view. Beyond the trees in the background lay the track that became today's Pertwee Drive.

127. Mills' butcher's and grocer's were the last occupiers of the shop which burnt down in 1939. South Woodham's unmade tracks would have been a challenge to the shop's delivery boy Jack Holden, pictured here in about 1930.

128. This row of six cottages was built for employees of the Woodham Ferris Brick Company on land owned by the company near Clementsgreen Creek. Although the cottages had fulfilled their original function by about 1908 they survived on the original Brickfields Road into the early 1970s.

129. Another of the many general stores in the village in the inter-war years was established by two sisters, Elizabeth and Mary Mudford, in 1927. It stood at the western end of Top Barn Lane on a site now occupied by 223 Hullbridge Road.

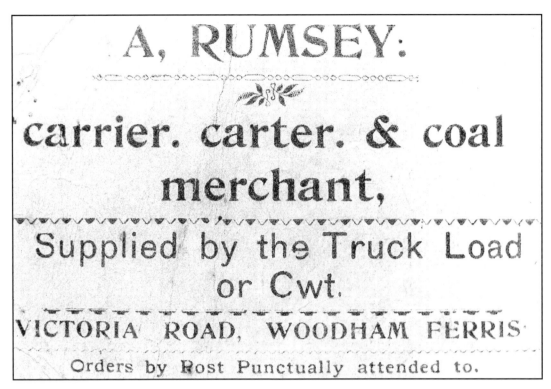

A, RUMSEY:

carrier. carter. & coal merchant,

Supplied by the Truck Load or Cwt.

VICTORIA ROAD, WOODHAM FERRIS.

Orders by Post Punctually attended to.

130. Unusually for a business venture in South Woodham Ferrers, the proprietor did not live on the premises. Arthur Rumsey's card, *c.*1912, is a reminder that the family lived in Victoria Road, more than half a mile from the depot (see illustration 132).

131. George Mudford moved to South Woodham Ferrers in 1918, and in the 1920s began building up his haulage and removal business. This Model T Ford truck was one of his earliest vehicles, pictured here with relatives aboard, and giving a literal meaning to the term 'family transport business'.

132. With donkey held firm in the iron grip of a formidable Mrs. Rumsey, Arthur Rumsey and family pose outside their business premises in about 1912. These premises stood on the southern side of the King Edwards Road – Hullbridge Road junction, on a site later occupied by South Woodham Dairy.

133. The Holden family's chickens were kept on land to the rear of their bungalow (below). Here in 1930 Les Holden poses with a cooperative fowl in front of the railway carriage henhouse.

134. One of the many small ventures established by Londoners who moved into the growing village in the 1920s was Henry Holden's boot and shoe repairing business. This bungalow is Claremont, which stood adjacent to St Mary's church in Hullbridge Road, and from where the business was run between 1924 and 1933.

135. The village's first garage, which is today's South Woodham Garage in Old Wickford Road, opened in the mid-1920s. This picture, showing petrol available at 1s. 2d. a gallon, dates from 1932.

Wickford – Burnham Road

136. In later years this rough, narrow track, pictured here at the turn of the century, became Wickford Road, the main route into the village from the west. The signpost stands at the junction with Creephedge Lane, whilst in the distance are the horse chestnut trees near Shaw Farm and Fenn Farm.

137. Curiously watching the photographer from the shadows of the trees at the entrance to Fenn Farm are two women, whose clothing suggests a pre-First World War date for this view of Wickford Road.

138.   This peaceful view of Wickford Road, in the 1930s, shows White's Café on the extreme left, which followed the example of *The Whalebone* by locating on this through route to capture passing trade.

139. South Woodham's building boom in the 1920s saw the construction of the village's first council houses in what is now Old Wickford Road. Near to the houses in this view, *c.*1930, is the café which burnt down in 1966.

140. This photograph from the late 1930s or early 1940s shows F. E. Buxton's builders' merchants on the left. South Woodham's first police office, established in 1936, stands beyond the white fence.

141.   Red Cottages, taken at about the turn of the century, shows part of the building in use as a shop. The adjacent highway appears to be little more than a single track width.

142.   Viewed from the embankment of the Maldon branch line, the eastern edge of the Champions Estate is marked by these properties. The upper length of this bypassed route now serves as today's Chadwick Road.

143.   An aerial view of William Tabrum's Copyhold on the junction with Hullbridge Road. It was originally a range of three timber-framed cottages dating from around the 17th century. Although extended and altered over the years, it is now officially protected as a building of historic or architectural interest.

144.   The road on the lower slopes of Bushy Hill provided views across the Crouch Valley as the river wound its way round
the northern edge of South Woodham Ferrers. The remains of the stretch of road in this picture now lie beneath the housing
development in Paston Close.

Hullbridge Road

145. The signpost at the top of a very rural-looking Hullbridge Road directs travellers to the railway station and Hullbridge ferry in this early 1920s view.

146. At the northern end of Hullbridge Road the adjoining land remained undeveloped in the inter-war period, and continued to provide a tree-lined entrance to the village. The twin roofs of the Smallholders' Hall are visible in the middle distance.

147.   Although by the 1920s Hullbridge Road had been divided for building plots along most of its length, farming land still abutted the road near the northern end of the village. It was here that farmer Eric Forrest made a site available for the erection of the Smallholders' Hall, and later for the village playing fields behind the hall.

148.   Before the construction of the shops in Warwick Parade the village centre, if it can be given such a grand title, was in the length of Hullbridge Road between the railway station and the Smallholders' Hall. All the buildings in this 1950s view near the junction with King Edward's Road are commercial or community premises.

149. This was the semi-rural scene into which newcomers arriving at the railway station would have walked in the early 1900s. The unsurfaced road comfortably coped with the horse-drawn traffic of the time.

150. By the mid-1930s the dramatic old oak tree (see 149) had been replaced by a rather more prosaic flagpole, much to the detriment of the street scene at this point.

151. The nucleus of buildings along this part of the road became a natural choice for the location of a doctor's premises. The occupiers of at least three of these cottages provided consulting rooms for the fondly remembered Dr. Frew who, from 1919, was the visiting doctor in the village for more than 40 years.

152. It is perhaps surprising that inter-war photographs of South Woodham Ferrers did not capture on film more of the 20,000 chickens which were reportedly around the village at that time. Approaching the level crossing from the left, however, in this 1930s photograph, can be seen a lone, less camera-shy, fowl.

153. With the mud of Clements Green Lane in the foreground, the beginnings of a new era are evident in the background. New fencing, building materials and sales office flagpole can be seen where Champions Way was being built by Cooper Estates in the mid-1960s.

154. This 1930s view of Hullbridge Road shows the ditches which once ran on each side of the road. The entrances over the ditch on the right were to the school (later Elmwood School annexe) and the new Baptist church.

155. Hullbridge Road, in some places, retained the appearance of a country lane with generous tree cover and grass verges long after the plotland development commenced. One of the plotland estate roads, later to become the eastern end of Pertwee Drive, passes between the houses on the left in this inter-war view.

156. The curiously named Tazzy Mazzy was a typical Essex weatherboarded cottage seen here in the early 1920s. Sadly this simple but pleasant building, which stood south of St Mary's Mission church, was destroyed by fire in 1931.

157. Meadowcroft, at the corner of Victoria Road, stood in a large garden and was acquired by Essex County Council in 1973 when land was being acquired for the new town project.

158. F. W. Deavin's shop, unlike its neighbours of the early 1920s, has survived into the 1990s. All these properties were built on plots designated for shops on the Eyotts sales plan.

159. Not surprisingly Hullbridge Road building plots proved more popular with purchasers than the newly laid-out estate roads. This inter-war view near the southern limit of development seems to capture the spirit of the times: an unregulated variety of buildings and unclipped verges providing homes for pioneers and for wildlife alike.

160. Oakdene near the southern end of development in Hullbridge Road stood adjacent to a dairy run by Eddie Lazell. Whilst today's dairy was being built on the old coalyard site near King Edward's Road in 1938, Oakdene provided the temporary home for the business shown here.

Around the Village

161. This stretch of road wending its muddy way towards Hullbridge Road in the distance is now lined by the neat gardens of Clements Green Lane. When photographed in the 1960s, the reason for the use of its locally adopted name of Mud Lane is somewhat evident.

162. This length of The Chase viewed towards the west, in 1966, was a long-established route to the southern side of the farmhouse and outbuildings at Champions Farm. It became an estate road in the 1895 Champions land sales plan to serve section 'A' of the estate.

163. The grass estate roads sustained by domestic ash and clinker from the grates of fronting properties were ill-suited to the demands and upheaval created by increased motor traffic and sewer-laying excavations. Residents of The Chase in the 1960s faced a long, mud-clinging walk to the surfaced pavements of Hullbridge Road in the distance.

164. In Victoria Road, about half a mile from the railway station, there were the isolated beginnings of a street of brick houses cheek by jowl with timber and asbestos properties seen here in 1972.

165.   One of the delightfully idiosyncratic buildings on the Eyotts Estate was Rose Cottage which from this angle would not have looked out of place in a London street of terraced houses.

166.   King Edward's Road, serving sections 'B' and 'C' of the Champions Hall Estate, was a pleasant grass track in the inter-war years. It developed into South Woodham's worst road in the 1970s as development along its length intensified and new estates were built on the amalgamated rear gardens of its long plots. It was properly surfaced in 1978.

Toward the New Town

167. A picture which says more than any description could about the wholesale change that was heralded by phase one of the 1970s new town project. The old rectilinear pattern of the Champions Estate is beginning to give way to a new order on the eastern side of the village.

Although some consolidation of the essentially scattered development had taken place in the pre-war years, much of the outlying area remained as a haphazard mixture of holiday homes, shacks, unmade tracks, smallholding and scrubland. The problems of this uneconomic land-use pattern were compounded by fragmented ownerships and during the Second World War, as in the Great War, the area became an obvious choice for the attentions of the War Agriculture Committee which was co-ordinating food production as part of the war effort. Almost 90 individual parcels of land comprising over 200 acres were acquired from owners of substantial sites and individual plot owners alike as the land was amalgamated to meet the needs of the time.

South Woodham Ferrers did not escape the austerity of the post-war years and there was no major change in the general pattern of gradual, piecemeal development. By 1960 the population had reached about 900 people. However, in the late 1950s a developer from Kent, Cooper Estates, had been obtaining options on considerable acreages of land in the village area with agreements to purchase within three years if planning permission for housing became available. Such consent was subsequently obtained and throughout the 1960s the village underwent a marked change in character as a number of new housing estates were built clustering round the station. By the end of that decade the population had more than quadrupled.

Although there was pressure for further expansion, the character of the area beyond the new estates presented insuperable problems for any private developer. Much of the land was owned by the Ministry of Agriculture and there was a large number of individual scattered plots, some of unknown ownership.

The increased housing demands in the south-east in the early 1970s led to investigations into the further expansion of South Woodham Ferrers. The site proved to be particularly attractive for a number of reasons. Expansion would not infringe green belt policies nor would it affect land of high agricultural or landscape value, the railway line, although much run down by this time, still provided a one hour link with London and in addition there were the recreational advantages offered by the riverside location.

A further important reason for the choice of South Woodham Ferrers for development and its expansion into a town of 18,000 people arose from the old plotland development surroundings of the village which Essex County Council, as promoters of the new town, described as 'consisting largely of scattered sub-standard dwellings without made up roads, services or other amenities'.[1]

The scale of the problem faced by the county council in its land amalgamation exercise became apparent when 229 individual plots of land were identified for acquisition of which more than ten per cent were of uncertain or unknown ownership.

Arguably the positive aspects of plotland development and life were inadequately addressed at this stage. Instead the area's problems and difficulties had become paramount and they prompted a drastic solution. Ironically it was to be the legacy of the plotland dream that was a determining factor in the decision that South Woodham Ferrers should again be the target of an influx of new settlers eager, as were those early plot purchasers, to enjoy the benefits that this corner of Essex appeared to offer.

1. *South Woodham Ferrers - Report of Public Inquiry*, Department of the Environment (1974), p.7.

168. Viewed from the north, today's Hamberts Road and Burnham Road cut through the remains of the Maldon branch line embankment in the foreground, whilst beyond lay the vacant sites of the industrial areas, secondary school and town centre.

The New Town

South Woodham Ferrers is not a 'new town' in the accepted sense of the term. Britain's post-war new towns, initially forming a ring round London, were run by autonomous development corporations and were established with a high level of input from the public sector to provide housing for people moving out of London. The South Woodham Ferrers scheme on the other hand was primarily a project established to meet a recognised demand for ready-serviced land for private house building purposes. No special body was set up to run the project and no special central government grants were made available. The project was run within normal local authority procedures and in an informal partnership with the private sector.

South Woodham's scale, too, stands in stark contrast to London's new towns: its target population of 18,000 represents about one quarter the size of those earlier towns. Indeed Essex County Council has distanced itself from the 'new town' label by describing the project as 'A New Riverside Country Town'.

As the town took shape it became apparent that the 'Country Town' image was particularly appropriate and that an environment very different to that provided by earlier developments in the area was being created. The 1960s estates of uninspired rows of speculative houses gave way to a greater variety of housing schemes containing design and layout elements and using external materials, which reflected those traditionally found in the longer established towns and villages of Essex.

This more varied and imaginative approach to housing design and layout was brought about by the county council's influential *A Design Guide for Residential Areas*, published in 1973, coincidentally the same year that the South Woodham Ferrers new town proposals were made public. The *Guide* introduced a new range of road standards and encouraged a better and more appropriate approach to the design of new residential development. The South Woodham Ferrers project became the first large-scale application of these new policies and, through its unique position as landowner as well as planning authority, the county council was well placed to ensure that the new standards were upheld.

Although a pilot development of 18 houses near Fenn Farm almost foundered and initial land releases were made in a depressed housing market, the project received a welcome boost when a superstore and related shops were opened in 1978 – well in advance of the expected increase in population. The architectural treatment of this first phase of the town centre, with its weatherboarded clock tower and selection of historical motifs, set the tone for later town centre developments which contributed in no small part to the town's particular character.

As well as its architectural contribution the early town centre development had an appreciable effect in encouraging house and land sales. By the mid-1980s new families were moving into the town at a rate of more than ten each week – a considerable rate of growth for the existing community to absorb, but one which also brought the advantages of increased facilities. The county council's innovative community school incorporating a secondary school, the town's library, multi-purpose hall and community rooms opened in the town centre in 1982 together with an inter-denominational church linked with church-aided schools. A health clinic, leisure facilities, public houses and further commercial premises each brought its own particular service and additional architectural contribution to the town centre, whilst after initial scepticism on the part of housebuilders, the new approach to house design and the tight urban spaces advocated in the *Design Guide* soon became strong selling points.

Although the town has largely succeeded in achieving the county council's basic planning aims, established at the commencement of the project, it is perhaps in achieving an unwritten and understated objective that particular success can be claimed. Rather than creating just another ordinary housing development, the public and private agencies concerned with the town's growth have succeeded in creating a place with a distinctive character which, as the town matures, should stand as a clear demonstration of what positive planning can achieve.

169. The formal commencement of engineering work on the new town project began on Tuesday 1 July 1975. In a field in the north-eastern corner of the development area, county council chairman Geoffrey Waterer symbolically cut the turf on the alignment of a new sewer in the £2¾ million phase one infrastructure contract.

170. The town's pilot project of 18 houses near Fenn Farm shows a distinct preoccupation with privacy in its design by the extensive use of high-level windows and blank wall areas.

171. With their front doors opening almost directly onto the footway, terraces of small houses recreate something of the character of village streets in many areas of the town. This development in Elliot Close was built in 1980-81.

172. As this view of the development in Melville Heath shows, small blocks of flats have been concentrated in higher density housing sites around the town centre. As well as providing much needed smaller homes in the town, these taller buildings fulfil a valuable role by helping to enclose the wider urban spaces created by the centre's distributor roads, roundabouts and car parks.

173. A wide range of housing densities has been adopted in the town. In a low density layout, such as this early development by Bovis Homes at Becket Way, landscaping is likely to make an increasingly important contribution to the appearance of what might otherwise be a rather ordinary housing scheme.

174. Children's play areas have been accommodated within the town's housing areas, as can be seen in this view east of Carisbrooke Drive (see illustration 68). Developers of adjoining sites contribute to a joint area at the boundary between their sites, thus producing a more effective open space.

175. Housebuilders soon recognised the marketability of that part of the Design Guide approach which encouraged variations in materials and external features to impart a degree of individuality to houses. These properties in Rivendell Vale (see illustration 80) are typical of the hundreds of three- and four-bedroomed houses built in the middle years of the project.

176. The eastern and western sectors of the town are served by a small sub-centre adjacent to each area's primary school. *The Curlew* public house and a shop adjacent to Chetwood School serve the western side; their styles reflect the variety found in nearby housing.

177.   It was not a pre-requisite of planning approval that housing in South Woodham Ferrers should follow the so-called 'neo-vernacular' style and by the 1980s developers were ready to break out of their self-imposed mould. This distinctive development in Inchbonnie Road exhibits influences of the 1930s Art-Deco style.

178.   The generally more adventurous architecture in the second (western) phase of the town found expression in a number of ways. A rich variety of height, depth, width, detailing and hues of pastel-painted brickwork has been used in this housing development in Bucklebury Heath.

179.   A development of 30 Dutch-gabled houses reflects the Flemish architectural influences found in East Anglia from the 16th century onwards. This was a brave move by builders Hey and Croft which brought additional variety to housing design in the town.

180.   The Church of the Holy Trinity accommodates Church of England, Roman Catholic and Methodist congregations. In a town centre which is rich in towers and cupolas it seems ironic that the town centre church itself does not make a bolder architectural statement.

181. Reminiscent of merchants' houses in a medieval town, these buildings on the eastern side of Market Square were built between 1988 and 1991 to accommodate shops, offices and a cinema.

182. The construction of a superstore in 1978 provided the town with a commercial and visual focal point. This early view along Heralds Way shows the superstore clocktower as originally built.

183. When the superstore was extended in 1985, the tower was increased in height by some two metres for improved visual effect, as the later view from Guild Way illustrates.

Bibliography

Edwards, A. C., *A History of Essex* (1978).

Essex County Council, *A Design Guide for Residential Area* (1973).

Fisher, G. J., *South Woodham Ferrers 1889-1939*, unpublished work.

Hardy, D. and Ward, C., *Arcadia for All* (1984).

Holden, L. A., *Where's Woodham Ferris?* (1988).

Morant, Rev. P., *The History and Antiquities of the County of Essex*, vol. II (1768).

Morris, J. ed., *Domesday Book - Essex* (1983).

Murphy, P. and Wilkinson, T. J., *The Hullbridge Basin Survey*, Interim Report No. 1 (1982).

Neale, C., *South Woodham Ferrers*, R.I.C.S. Case Study (1984).

Reaney, P. H., *The Place Names of Essex* (1969).

South Woodham Ferrers Women's Institute, *Our Village* (1965).

Swindale, D. L., *Branch Line to Southminster* (1981).

Turner, M. J., *Mill Hill to Overshot Bridge – A Short History of Bicknacre & Woodham Ferrers*.

The Victoria History of the County of Essex, vol. I (1903).

Waterworth, F., *A Short History of South Woodham Ferrers* (1978).

Woricker, M. and J., *The History of Woodham Ferrers*.

Various issues of *Essex County Chronicle*, *Essex Countryside*, *Essex Weekly News*, *Link – A Community Magazine for South Woodham Ferrers*.